SCHOLASTIC

Scrambled Sentences
SIGHT WORDS

40 Hands-on Pages That Boost Early Reading & Handwriting Skills

Pig took some books with him.

Pig took some books with him.

New York • Toronto • London • Auckland • Sydney

Mexico City • New Delhi • Hong Kong • Buenos Aires

Written and produced by Immacula A. Rhodes
Cover design by Tannaz Fassihi
Interior design by Jaime Lucero
Cover and interior illustrations by Doug Jones

ISBN: 978-1-338-11297-9

2 3 4 5 6 7 8 9 10   40   23 22 21 20 19 18 17

Contents

Scrambled Sentences Activity Pages

Introduction

Welcome to Scrambled Sentences: Sight Words!

The 40 activity pages in this book were developed to give children an engaging and fun way to practice recognizing the top 80 high-frequency words found on the Dolch Basic Sight Word Vocabulary List and to put words together to create, read, and write sentences. In addition to boosting early reading and writing skills, the activities also give children lots of opportunities to hone their fine motor and visual skills.

On each page, children cut out and unscramble a set of words to create a sentence that describes a picture. The sentence includes targeted sight words for that page, giving children repeated practice in recognizing and reading those words. Once children have arranged and glued the words into a sentence, they write that sentence on the provided line and then color the picture. As they do the activity,

children perform a number of tasks, such as cutting, gluing, writing, and coloring, which help build and strengthen their fine motor abilities.

You can use the scrambled sentences with the whole class, in small groups, or as the focus of a one-on-one lesson. You can also place them in a learning center for children to use independently or in pairs. The activities are ideal for children of all learning styles, as well as for ELL students, and for RTI instruction. And best of all, they support children in meeting the standards for Reading Foundational Skills for grades K–2. (See below.)

Connections to the Standards

Print Concepts
Demonstrate understanding of the organization and basic features of print.

Phonological Awareness
Demonstrate understanding of spoken words, syllables, and sounds (phonemes).

Phonics and Word Recognition
Read common high-frequency words by sight.

Fluency
Read with sufficient accuracy and fluency to support comprehension.

Source: © Copyright 2010 National Governors Association Center for Best Practices and Council of Chief State School Officers. All rights reserved.

How to Use the Scrambled Sentences

Materials (for each child)

- scrambled sentence page
- scissors
- glue
- pencil
- crayons

Completing a scrambled sentence page is easy and fun. To begin, distribute copies of the activity page for the sight words you want to teach. Point out the target words on the page and read them aloud. Then have children do the following:

1. Cut out the word strip at the bottom of the page. Then cut apart the words.

2. Put the words in order to make a sentence that goes with the picture. Glue the words in the sentence box.

3. Write the sentence on the line.

4. Color the picture.

Note: *See the Scrambled Sentences List on page 7 to check the correct word sequence for the sentence on each activity page.*

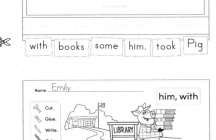

Teaching Tips

Use these handy tips to ensure children get the most from the scrambled sentence activities.

- **Provide a model:** Display a completed scrambled sentence page. Then demonstrate, step by step, how to complete the activity, including the use of think-alouds to model how to figure out individual words and the sentence.

- **Focus on the target words:** Have children identify each of the target sight words, read the word aloud, and color the word.

- **Use the clues:** Point out that children can use the picture to help figure out individual words and what the sentence should say. They can also use what they know about sentence features to sequence the words: The first word of a sentence begins with a capital letter and the last word ends with a punctuation mark.

- **Reinforce reading at every step:** Have children read each word after cutting apart the words, before and after gluing the words in place, and after writing the sentence. As children read the sentence, encourage the use of an appropriate inflection for that type of sentence (statement, question, exclamation).

Scaffolding Suggestions

Provide support as children's needs dictate. Here are a few suggestions.

Reading

- Display each word and help children sound it out. You might also read the word aloud and have children repeat.

- Point out each target sight word and ask children to read the word aloud, repeating it several times.

- Provide the correct word order for the sentence. As needed, work individually with children to put the sentence together, one word at a time.

- Model reading the sentence aloud and have children repeat.

Writing

- Have children practice writing the target words on the line, instead of writing the full sentence. If needed, write the words on the line in advance and have children trace them.

- Ahead of time, lightly pencil in the sentence on the writing line. Then have children trace the sentence.

TIP

For children with less developed cutting skills, cut out each individual word in advance. Or cut out the word strip and have children cut apart the words.

Ways to Use the Scrambled Sentences

- Learning center activity
- Whole-class instruction
- Small-group instruction
- One-on-one lesson
- Partner activity
- Individual seatwork
- Morning starter
- End-of-the-day wrap up
- Take-home practice

More Uses

- Label a folder with each child's name. Encourage children to place their completed scrambled sentence pages in their folder. Have children use the pages for review and to practice reading.

- Help children compile their pages into a booklet to take home and share.

Customized Scrambled Sentences

Use the template on page 48 to create your own scrambled sentences. First, choose a pair of sight words to feature on the page. Print the words in the skill box at the upper-right side of the page. Then create a sentence that features both sight words. For best results, limit the word count to six or fewer words and the total letter count to 22 or fewer letters. Draw a simple sketch to represent the sentence and write the words in random order on the strip at the bottom of the page. (Be sure to include a capital letter for the first word of the sentence and punctuation with the last word.) Separate the words with vertical cutting lines, leaving space between each one. Then copy a class supply of the page to distribute to children.

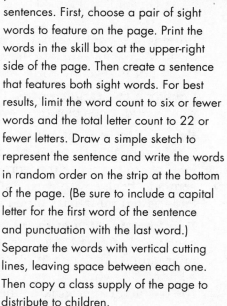

Scrambled Sentences List

Use this handy list as a reference for checking the correct word sequence for the sentence on each activity page.

the, to *(page 8)*
Turtle goes to the zoo.

a, and *(page 9)*
Frog and a toad
ate cookies.

I, you *(page 10)*
I have some treats
for you.

he, it *(page 11)*
He knows it will go in!

in, of *(page 12)*
Lots of bees were
in there.

but, was *(page 13)*
Snail was slow but
she won!

said, she *(page 14)*
Ann said she had
a surprise.

his, on *(page 15)*
A bird was on his hat!

for, that *(page 16)*
Please get that kite
for me.

had, they *(page 17)*
Dog hoped they had
more paint.

at, her *(page 18)*
Kim found her cubby
at school.

him, with *(page 19)*
Pig took some books
with him.

is, up *(page 20)*
Squirrel is going up
the tree.

all, look *(page 21)*
Come look at all the fish!

some, there
(page 22)
Duck puts some hay
in there.

go, out *(page 23)*
Cow is ready to go out.

as, we *(page 24)*
We are as quiet as mice.

am, be *(page 25)*
I am going to be tall!

have, play
(page 26)
He will play then
have lunch.

down, little
(page 27)
A little bird flew
down here.

do, what *(page 28)*
What will the owl do?

can, see *(page 29)*
Bee can see the flowers
now!

could, not *(page 30)*
Cat could not reach the
toy.

did, when *(page 31)*
When did you get new
shoes?

so, were *(page 32)*
The chicks were so sleepy.

get, this *(page 33)*
Rabbit wants to get
this one.

my, them *(page 34)*
I saw them eat my
crackers!

like, would
(page 35)
Horse would like an apple.

me, one *(page 36)*
Can you give me one
lollipop?

will, yes *(page 37)*
Will her mom say yes?

big, came *(page 38)*
Lion came to the big cave.

ask, went *(page 39)*
Bob went to ask for help.

are, long *(page 40)*
These dogs are very long!

come, if *(page 41)*
I will come if I can.

no, now *(page 42)*
Monkey has no
bananas now.

blue, very *(page 43)*
Whale lives in very
blue water.

an, just *(page 44)*
Jill just saw an ostrich!

over, ride *(page 45)*
Crab can ride over
the waves.

its, your *(page 46)*
Your hamster likes
its ball.

into, red *(page 47)*
Goat goes into the
red barn.

Name _____

the, to

Cut.
Glue.
Write.
Color.

ZOO

LUNCH

Glue words here.

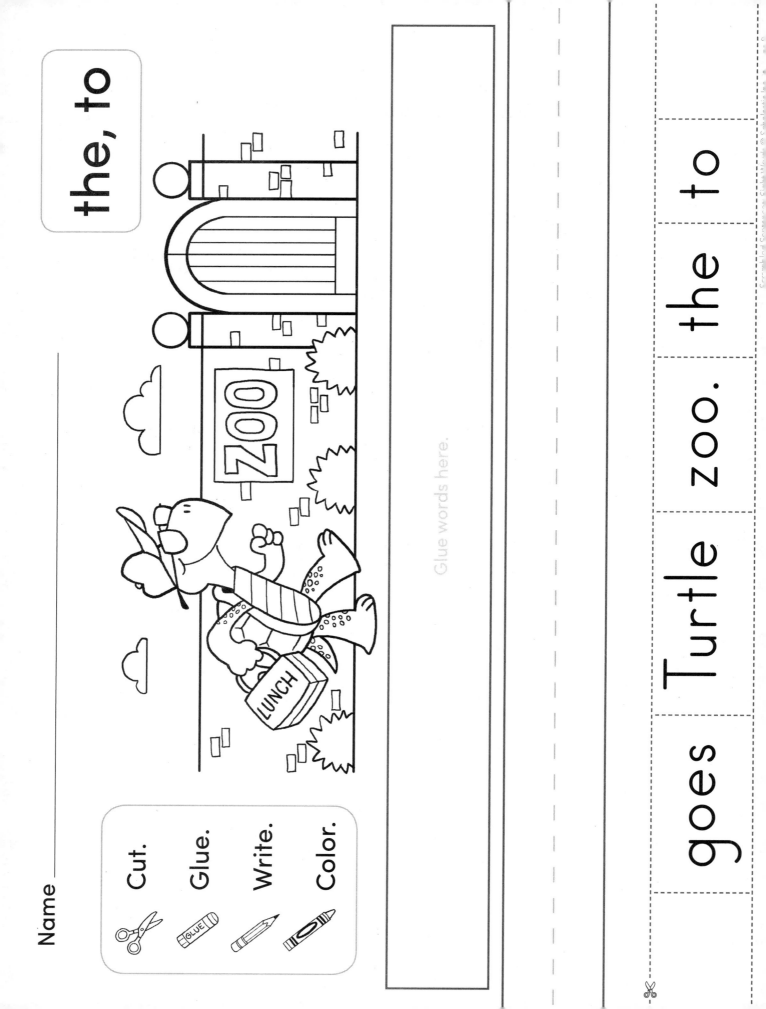

goes Turtle zoo. the to

Name _____

Cut.

Glue.

Write.

Color.

Glue words here.

✂ -

cookies. | and | ate | a | Frog | toad

Name _____

Cut.

Glue.

Write.

Color.

PAMPERED PUP TASTY TREATS

Glue words here.

treats | for | I | have | you. | some

Name _____

Cut.

Glue.

Write.

Color.

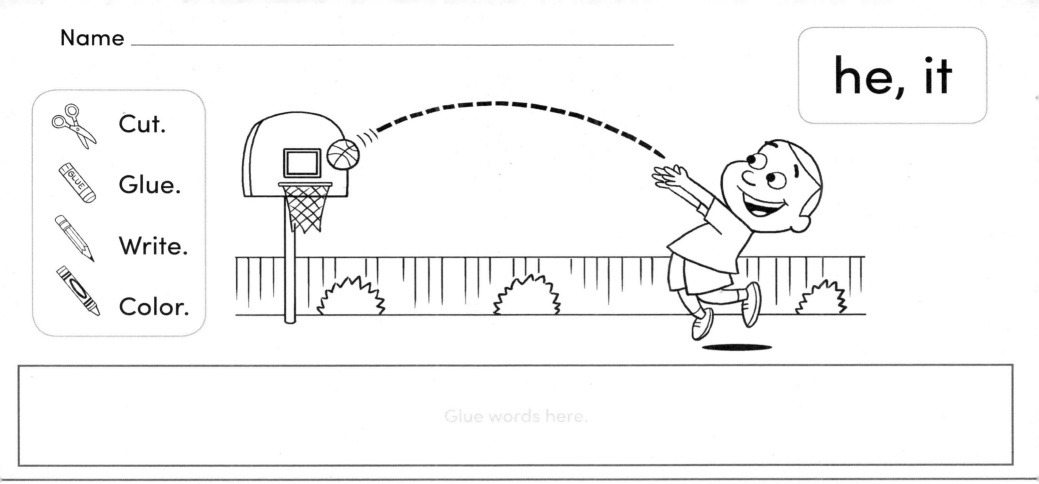

Glue words here.

✂ -

| He | it | knows | go | will | in! |

| bees | there. | were | Lots | in | of |

Glue words here.

in, of

Cut.
Glue.
Write.
Color.

Name

Name _____

Cut.

Glue.

Write.

Color.

FINISH

Glue words here.

---

slow | won! | but | Snail | she | was

Name _____

Cut.

Glue.

Write.

Color.

Glue words here.

---

said | Ann | surprise. | had | she | a

Name _____

Cut.

Glue.

Write.

Color.

Glue words here.

✂ ------------------------------------

hat! | bird | his | was | A | on

for, that

✂ Cut.

🖍 Glue.

✏ Write.

🖍 Color.

Glue words here.

_____

_____

✂ | kite | for | Please | get | me. | that

Name _____

Cut.

Glue.

Write.

Color.

Glue words here.

- -

Dog | they | hoped | more | had | paint.

Name _____

Cut.

Glue.

Write.

Color.

Glue words here.

✂ her | school. | cubby | Kim | at | found

him, with

Cut.

Glue.

Write.

Color.

LIBRARY

Glue words here.

with | books | some | him. | took | Pig

Name _____

is, up

Cut.

Glue.

Write.

Color.

Glue words here.

✂ ----- is | Squirrel | tree. | up | going | the

all, look

Cut.

Glue.

Write.

Color.

FISH

Glue words here.

✂ -

fish! | look | the | at | Come | all

Name _____

Cut.

Glue.

Write.

Color.

Glue words here.

✂ hay | puts | Duck | some | there. | in

Name _____

go, out

Cut.

Glue.

Write.

Color.

Glue words here.

✂ --

| Cow | to | is | ready | out. | go |

Name _____

 Cut.

Glue.

Write.

Color.

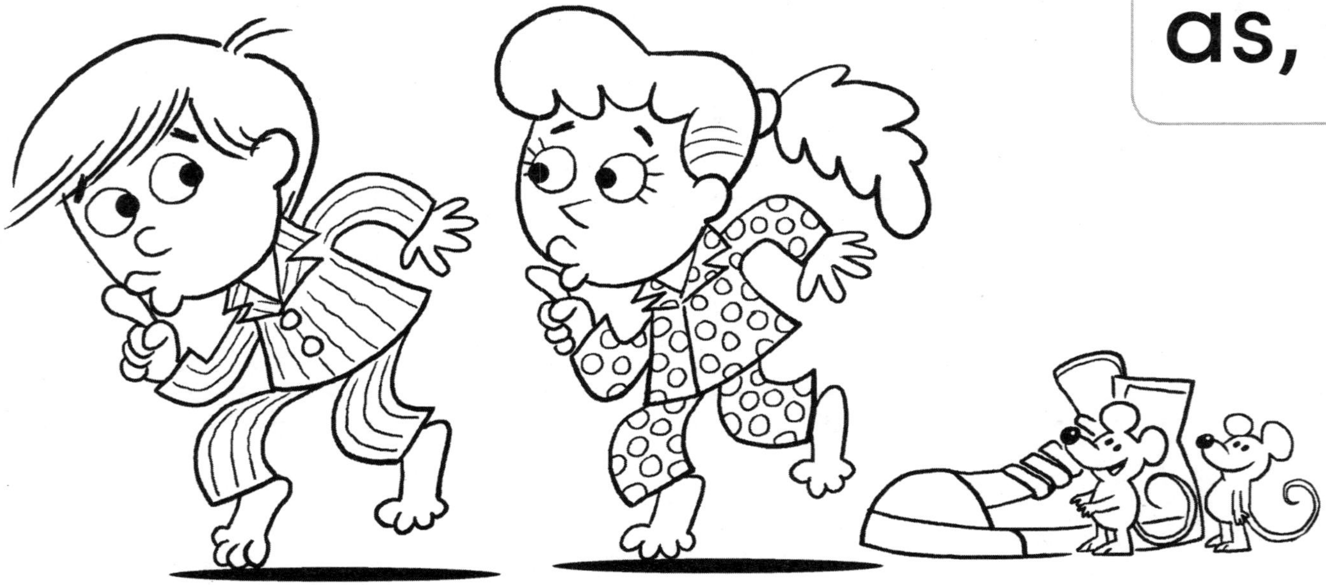

Glue words here.

✂ -

as | mice. | quiet | We | as | are

am, be

Cut.

Glue.

Write.

Color.

WE ARE GROWING!

6 FEET

5 FEET

4 FEET

3 FEET

GIRAFFE

ELEPHANT

ZEBRA

Glue words here.

be | to | going | tall! | am | I

Name _____

have, play

- Cut.
- Glue.
- Write.
- Color.

Glue words here.

✂ will | He | lunch. | then | play | have

Name _____

Cut.

Glue.

Write.

Color.

Glue words here.

here. | little | down | bird | A | flew

Name _____

Cut.

Glue.

Write.

Color.

Glue words here.

owl | do? | What | will | the

Name _____

Cut.

Glue.

Write.

Color.

Glue words here.

Bee | see | can | flowers | the | now!

Name _____

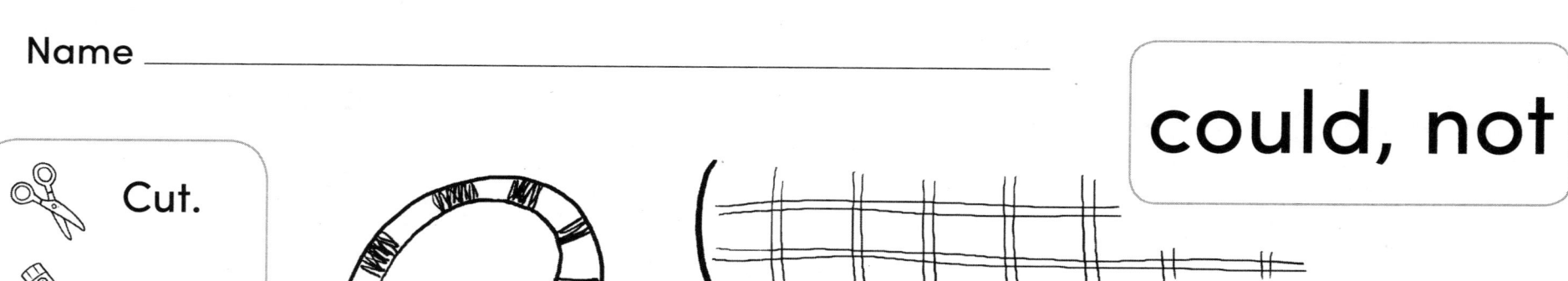

- Cut.
- Glue.
- Write.
- Color.

Glue words here.

- -

✂ -

| not | toy. | reach | Cat | the | could |

Name _____

did, when

Cut.

Glue.

Write.

Color.

Glue words here.

new | get | you | shoes? | did | When

Scrambled Sentences: Sight Words © Scholastic Inc. • page 31

so, were

Cut.

Glue.

Write.

Color.

Glue words here.

✂

chicks | The | sleepy. | were | so

Name _____

Cut.

Glue.

Write.

Color.

BIKE SALE !

Glue words here.

✂ one. | wants | this | to | Rabbit | get

my, them

Cut.

Glue.

Write.

Color.

Glue words here.

✂ eat | my | I | saw | crackers! | them

Name _____

like, would

Cut.

Glue.

Write.

Color.

Glue words here.

✂ -

Horse | like | would | an | apple.

Name ____________________

me, one

Cut.

Glue.

Write.

Color.

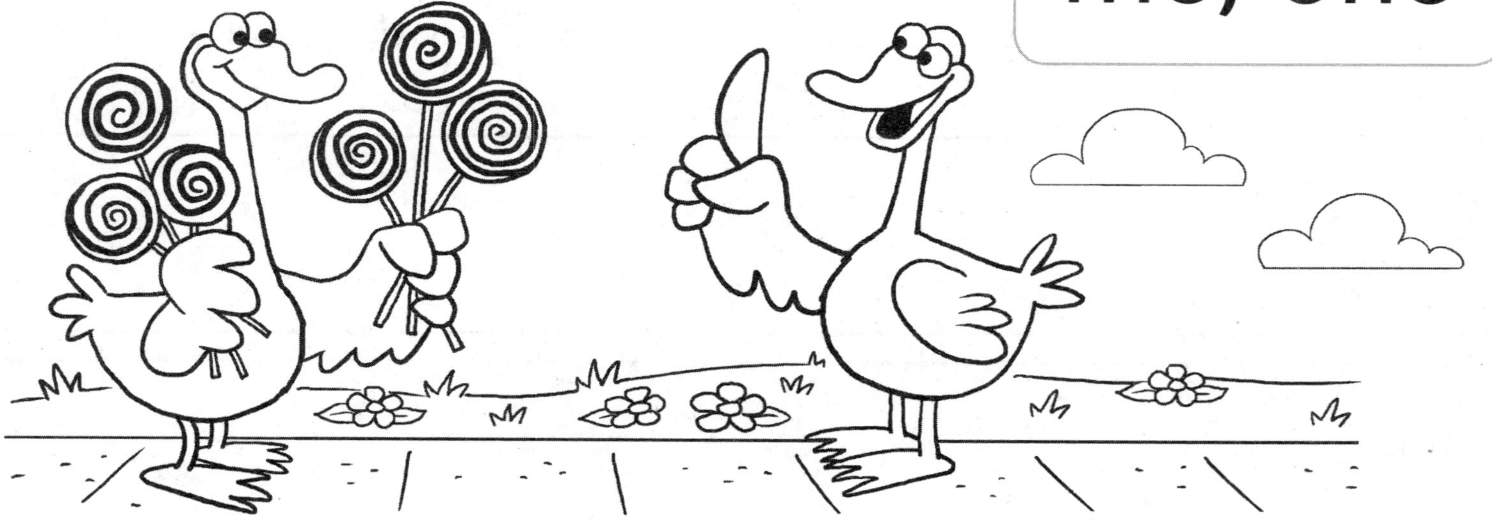

Glue words here.

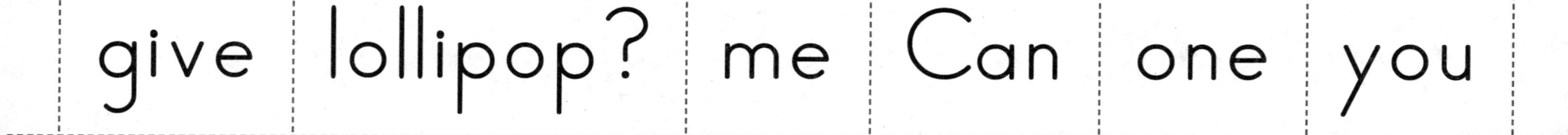

give	lollipop?	me	Can	one	you

will, yes

Cut.

Glue.

Write.

Color.

MAY I KEEP THEM?

FREE KITTENS

Glue words here.

✂ --

yes? | say | mom | her | Will

big, came

Cut.

Glue.

Write.

Color.

LIONS ONLY

Glue words here.

---

came | Lion | cave. | the | to | big

Name _____

Cut.

Glue.

Write.

Color.

TIRE STORE →

Glue words here.

- -

✂ -

| help. | went | for | to | Bob | ask |

Name _____

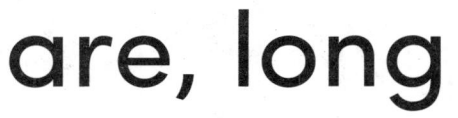
are, long

 Cut.

 Glue.

 Write.

 Color.

Glue words here.

are | very | These | long! | dogs

Name _____

✂ Cut.

🧴 Glue.

✏ Write.

🖍 Color.

CAN YOU COME?

YOU ARE INVITED TO A PARTY!

Glue words here.

will | I | if | come | can. | I

no	bananas	Monkey	now.	has

Glue words here.

no, now

Cut.	Glue.	Write.	Color.

BANANAS

Name _____

Cut.

Glue.

Write.

Color.

Glue words here.

- -

blue | very | in | water. | lives | Whale

Name _____

Cut.

Glue.

Write.

Color.

Glue words here.

✂ -

| just | Jill | an | saw | ostrich! |

Name _____

Cut.

Glue.

Write.

Color.

Glue words here.

✂ waves. | can | the | ride | Crab | over

Name _____

Cut.

Glue.

Write.

Color.

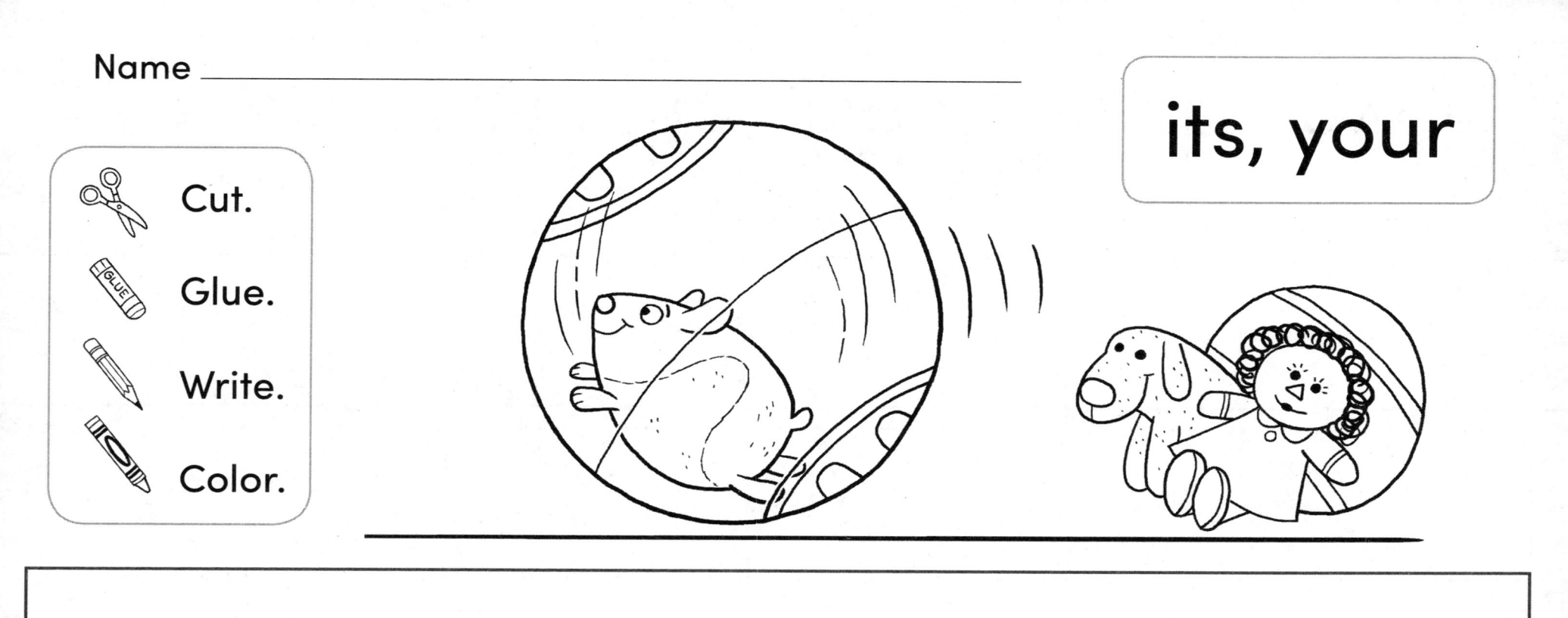

Glue words here.

✂ -

| its | ball. | Your | hamster | likes |

Name _____

Cut.

Glue.

Write.

Color.

Glue words here.

---

the | into | goes | red | Goat | barn.

Name _____

Cut.

Glue.

Write.

Color.

Glue words here.